QuickBooks

The Quick and Easy QuickBooks Guide for Your Small Business – Accounting and Bookkeeping

QuickBooks

© **Copyright 2016 - All rights reserved.**

direct or indirect, which are incurred as a result of the use of information contained within this document, including, but not limited to, —errors, omissions, or inaccuracies.

QuickBooks

Table of Contents

Introduction

Running a small business can be very fulfilling, yet at the same time quite challenging. It may seem like you are always desperately trying to juggle several balls at the same time. You must have a number of key skills that can help you keep everything in check so that your focus is maintained on the important activities.

One of the main reasons why someone sets up their own small business is to create opportunities for making money. A small business also offers you the chance to use the skills you have to engage in an economic activity that perfectly suits you. Since money is one of the motivating factors for a small business existing in the first place, it is crucial that accounting and bookkeeping be taken very seriously. The financial health of your business must be maintained if it is to succeed.

This book is written with the intention of giving you all the information you will need to learn how to use QuickBooks effectively for your small business. The book starts off with a brief introduction of what QuickBooks are and why you need them for your business. This chapter should be read keenly if you are just starting out with QuickBooks. You are likely to learn some basic information that will help you understand how to make the best use of this type of accounting software.

There are a number of different versions of QuickBooks available in the market. Before you rush out and grab whatever you can find, or simply use what your friend recommended, it would be advisable to go through Chapter 3 of this book. You will learn all you need to know about QuickBooks versions and how to choose the one that will help your business the most.

Not many people are familiar with how to use accounting software properly. This makes navigating through the system a bit complicated for most business owners, which is why this book takes the time to teach you how to use QuickBooks for the various purposes that are necessary for running an effective and successful business. This is the part that you should pay close attention to if you want to avoid some of the common mistakes business owners make with QuickBooks. There are also some tips, tricks, and shortcuts that always come in handy when you want to speed up your bookkeeping.

This book is written in an easy-to-read manner with minimal technical jargon. This is to help you understand what to do in every step. You can read the chapters individually instead of going through the book from cover to cover. If you have some experience in using QuickBooks, you may simply jump to the section you are keen on and take it from there. However, it is recommended that beginners start with chapter one and work their way chapter by chapter.

Enjoy the book!

Chapter 1: What is QuickBooks?

It is easy to find yourself overwhelmed by all the financial management responsibilities that come with running a small business. Keeping track of everything can be quite cumbersome. For this reason, most businesses are nowadays using accounting software to help in managing their business's finances.

QuickBooks is a set of accounting software solutions that are designed to help small business owners effectively and accurately organize their payroll, sales, inventory, and other accounting needs. This type of software can be used by just about anyone, as it does not require much accounting experience.

In other words, QuickBooks help you keep track of the income and expenditure of your business, generate reports and invoices, process credit card payments, and handle any other basic accounting processes.

Brief Background

The QuickBooks software package is a product developed and marketed by Intuit Inc. It is primarily targeted at small business owners, the majority of whom have no formal accounting experience. This has led to its massive popularity among small and medium-sized companies.

When QuickBooks accounting software was initially released, it did not meet the security and conventional accounting standards that the majority of professional accountants desired. However, QuickBooks has come a long way in terms of improving its features and security controls. It now has double-entry as well as full audit trail functionalities.

Intuit has also released more versions of QuickBooks accounting software, ranging from the basic package for beginners to the Pro version for more advanced users. There is also an industry-specific version that is designed for whatever business type you own. Medium-sized businesses have also been catered for by the release of a QuickBooks accounting package designed with an array of advanced features.

Features of QuickBooks Software

QuickBooks now offers a number of web-based features, such as remote access, online banking, e-payment capabilities, remote payroll assistance, Google Maps integration, and may other useful features. You can also track your employee's time, as well as import Excel spreadsheets. QuickBooks is now configured to run on both Windows OS as well Mac OS.

Factors to Consider For QuickBooks First-Timers

If you happen to be somewhat familiar with QuickBooks and understand how to use it, then this chapter is not for you. You can go ahead and skip this part. However, if you are using this accounting software for the first time, there are certain things you need to consider if you want to survive your initial interaction with QuickBooks.

1. Keep your business and personal accounts separate

QuickBooks provides a really useful service by allowing you to sync your checking account with the software. Whatever transactions you perform are automatically displayed and no manual filling in of information is required. However, if you are in the habit of using money in the business account for personal use, this feature can be a problem for your business. It is recommended that you have an account for business and another one for personal use.

2. Don't use estimates and invoices at first

Though the estimates and invoices features are very useful, avoid using them until you know more about QuickBooks. Why? Whenever you use these features, your accounting activity is automatically posted in QuickBooks. It is recommended that beginners create estimates and

3

invoices on a separate program, for example, MS Word, and then manually enter that data into QuickBooks. When you have understood how QuickBooks generates these amounts, then you can go ahead and use the QuickBooks Estimates and Invoices features.

3. Ask for help from a professional QuickBooks advisor

If you make a bad error and you don't know how to solve it, you should consider looking for help. Intuit has a system that enables you to find a QuickBooks Pro advisor in your local area. If you cannot afford to hire a professional, or simply don't feel like dealing with one, you can browse Intuit's Support Database for a solution.

Chapter 2: Why Your Business Needs QuickBooks

As a business owner, you understand just how important proper bookkeeping is for your business. You may have been keeping your books the traditional way – using pen and paper – but times have changed, and so have government regulations.

You may be thinking about acquiring an accounting software system for your business. You may have even considered different types of software in the market. But then the question is why should you use QuickBooks and not any other software package? Is QuickBooks really necessary for your business? What is so special about QuickBooks anyway?

Reasons for Maintaining an Accounting System

Before we look at why QuickBooks are the right solution for your business accounting needs, let's first ask why an accounting system is important.

There are two essential reasons why your business needs to maintain an accounting system. The first is government regulations. The government requires that businesses use a logical (easily understandable) accounting system that shows how much money it has made. This is meant to enable the computation of taxable income.

Now, it is understandable if you think that the government is simply a big leech trying to suck your profits in the form of ever-increasing taxes. You may even try to ignore this requirement altogether. However, this is never a good idea, and plenty a business owner has ended up on the wrong side of the law. You risk a fine or worse – jail time.

Fortunately, you are a law-abiding citizen and therefore we move on to the second reason why your business needs an accounting system. Believe it or not, but without a decent accounting system, your business will find it very difficult to succeed. You may be a great money manager, but running a successful business requires you to accurately measure and record your income and expenditure. It is the only way to determine whether your business is making profits or losses.

A good accounting system enables you to know the financial health of your business. You have to keep track of the products and services that are making you the most money, the customers that are bringing in the big bucks, and those who aren't.

Accounting and bookkeeping may seem like a tiresome and money-draining chore, but every business owner needs a good accounting system. Your success – and maybe your freedom – depends on it!

What QuickBooks Does

The truth is that QuickBooks make your life easier. How? By helping you to record all your common business transactions in a systematic manner. QuickBooks uses an interface, called a window, which enables you to fill in important information for various transactions. For example, when recording information about a check you want to pay out, all you have to do is fill in the date, amount, and the entity you want to pay. The window you see on your screen resembles an actual check. It is the same with every other financial transaction document you regularly use. An invoice window looks like an actual invoice, and all you have to do is fill in the blanks.

One of the greatest things about QuickBooks is that every financial detail captured in a particular window, from checks to invoices, is used to populate a profit and loss report that you can use to determine the financial state of your business.

QuickBooks makes your accounting process simpler and less time-consuming. Filling in data about transactions into a few windows allows you to quickly calculate whatever financial information you need. You can automatically create a balance sheet for any time period, whenever you need one. QuickBooks also helps you track client payments and inventory.

QuickBooks also has the capability to print out forms, such as invoices, containing all the information you filled in. They also come in handy when you need to do some electronic billing and banking. You can quickly email your clients an invoice, thus saving money and time. You are also able to share your bank account details with most large banks, therefore enabling you to send funds and pay suppliers electronically.

Reasons for Using QuickBooks

If you are looking for a great accounting system for your business, then QuickBooks is the best way to go. QuickBooks is the most widely used accounting software package on the globe. There are millions of businesses that are currently using QuickBooks as the foundation of their system, and its popularity is evident.

Here is why you should choose QuickBooks for your business:

QuickBooks is easy to use: What sets QuickBooks apart from its competitors is its ease of use. All you have to do is fill in information into a window that looks like your average financial form. As a businessperson, you are probably already familiar with forms like checks, invoices, purchase orders and the like. You don't need any special training or an accounting background to use this software package, unlike other accounting programs. In fact,

QuickBooks has become so popular that rival accounting software systems have copied its simplicity. The only downside to QuickBooks level of simplicity is that it does not have adequate in-built control mechanisms provided by your conventional accounting system. This means that your financial information may not be as safe as it would normally be, though it has to be said that these security controls tend to make the system more complicated for the average user.

QuickBooks is affordable: Before QuickBooks, businesses relied on traditional accounting systems that were very expensive, somewhere in the range of thousands of dollars. Nowadays, there are a number of versions of QuickBooks available in the market. All you need is a few hundred dollars to get a basic QuickBooks system up and running.

QuickBooks is widely available and known everywhere: Almost every accountant you talk to knows about QuickBooks. Almost every business owner either has heard of or knows how to use QuickBooks. The average freelancer is aware of QuickBooks, even if they might have never used the software. There are even QuickBooks classes being taught in local colleges. This is a testament to the ubiquity of QuickBooks. This is unlike other accounting programs that only a few accountants or business owners may know how to use. The fact that QuickBooks is easy to use and cheap makes it well-known and widely used.

Chapter 3: QuickBooks Versions for Small Businesses

When QuickBooks was first released, small businesses could only use the one version that was available. Today, there are several different versions of QuickBooks that business owners can use for accounting and bookkeeping purposes. There are also some QuickBooks versions that are very specific to certain industries.

The question that needs to be asked is this – How do you know which one to choose? These different versions are priced differently and offer a variety of applications. In this chapter, you will learn the different versions of QuickBooks and how to decide which one is perfect for your business needs. Though some are well-suited for the majority of small businesses, it is still important to understand what is available to you prior to investing in a particular solution.

QuickBooks for Mac

This version of QuickBooks is well-suited for a company whose computers all run on Mac. The Mac version of QuickBooks comes in a software package that is quite different from all the other versions, which use the Windows operating system.

QuickBooks Mac is designed to run on an interface that is specific for a Mac framework. This means that accessing the diverse sections and modules requires a user who is familiar with a Mac system. Though the initial versions of QuickBooks Mac were a bit unfriendly for users, the recent versions have greatly improved user experience and feel more like Mac applications.

QuickBooks for Mac has the following features:

- When it's set up the right way, it can be fun and easy to use, especially when performing online banking.

- It allows you to share your records and files with users running on a Windows system.

- It enables the user to design nice invoices that can be emailed together with a link that customers simply click to speed up cash payments.

- The accounting software also uses an online payroll that is able to sync data, thus negating the need for entering complex paychecks.

- It has a limited job costing functionality.

QuickBooks for Mac tends to develop bugs here and there, though it usually works well. The challenge with this software is in setting it up properly. There are also very few apps that are compatible with it, and collaboration with your bookkeeper is not easy at all. If you have the option of choosing between QuickBooks for Mac and online accounting software, go for the online version.

QuickBooks Online Edition

An online version of QuickBooks was released to suit those business professionals who wanted to access QuickBooks on–the–go. The online version is also great if you want to pay for the software whenever you need to rather than having to upgrade a desktop version. If you are a businessman or consultant who is constantly on the move, then QuickBooks Online should work well for you.

One of the best advantages of using QuickBooks Online is compatibility with all kinds of platforms. This is because the software is hosted and run on Intuit servers rather than an individual laptop, desktop, or mobile device. This makes sure that your data is secure and protected while ensuring that you make use of the latest software version. QuickBooks Online also has a set of features that are distinct from the desktop versions available. You can also retrieve your files anywhere and at any time, as long as you have access to the Internet. On the other hand, it is more expensive to use than the desktop application if you consider the charges on an annual basis.

QuickBooks Online provides the following features:

- Payroll management

- Creating invoices and estimates

- Sending estimates, reports, and invoices

- Sharing data with accountants

- Tracking sales, sales tax, payments, and inventory

- Creating more than 100 customizable accounting reports

QuickBooks Online comes in the following five versions:

1. Online Simple Start

This version does not contain many of the above useful features, hence its name. It is a basic application that is primarily used by sole proprietors and small business owners who may not need the advanced features.

It is simple to learn and use, and is a suitable long-term solution for freelancers, startups, and individual contractors. It is also available on Android, iPad, and iPhone apps, thus making it convenient for use for small business owners on the move.

There are menu links and tabs that help you find which kind of transaction you want to engage in. Due to its simplistic design, it may not have much value for businesses that want advanced or complex transactions. Online Simple Start comes with the following features:

- Creation and customization of invoices

- Tracking and reporting sales, taxes, and expenses

- Customization of business reports, for example, profit and loss, sales, and balance sheets

- Preparation of estimates

- Storage of client contacts

- Electronic payment of bills

The purpose of creating this version is to get small businesses to use the service for a fee as they test the waters. Once you realize that this version is inadequate for your business needs, you are expected to upgrade to a more useful version – of course at an extra cost.

2. Online Essentials

This version is slightly better than Online Simple Start, but it is still considered a basic accounting service. However, Essentials allows you to run your small business using the normal bookkeeping features. Most of the features that a normal business requires are still lacking, though. Online Essentials does not offer you features like billing by customer, budgeting and planning, inventory tracking, class tracking, tracking multiple locations, or creating purchase orders.

3. Online Essentials with Payroll

This is a similar version to the one above. The only difference is that it offers your business an online payroll service.

4. Online Plus

This online version of QuickBooks contains all the features that Essentials does not. If you decide to use QuickBooks over the Internet, then this is the version you need to go for. The majority of small business owners who opt for this version seem to be satisfied with what it has to offer. Online Plus provides the accounting requirements that any small business would need on a regular basis. In case your business has more complicated bookkeeping requirements, it is recommended that you get yourself a desktop software solution.

5. Online Plus with Payroll

This is a similar version to the one above. The only difference is that it offers your business a payroll service.

QuickBooks Pro Edition

Without a doubt, this is the QuickBooks version that users love the most. Why? The reason is that QuickBooks Pro offers the most comprehensive business accounting features that any company can use, all for a reasonable fee.

If your small business is being run on the Windows platform, you should opt for either QuickBooks Pro or the more advanced QuickBooks Premier.

These are the features that QuickBooks Pro offers:

- Step-by-step tutorials

- Supports three simultaneous users

- Tracking of payments, expenses, bills, and inventory

- Tracking time and expenses related to a specific customer

- Tracking sales, sales tax, and client accounts

- Batch invoicing

- Managing payroll

- Accepting credit cards

- Creating customizable reports, invoices, and estimates

QuickBooks Premier

This particular version is designed to fit whatever industry your business operates in. You are required to choose and buy the version that will suit your specific industry, for example, general business, retail, wholesale, manufacturing, contractors, professional services, or non-profit.

QuickBooks Pro offers a customization feature that the other versions do not, and its interface changes to display a language that is specific to your industry. For example, if you work in a non-profit organization, "customers" are displayed as "donors." Even the way reports are provided is customized to suit the industry your business operates in.

QuickBooks Premier provides users with additional features to what the Pro version has, such as:

- Reporting that is specific to your industry

- Tracking your costs for inventory and finished products

- Creating track-back and sales orders

- Forecasting of sales and expenses

- Business planning tools

- Supports five simultaneous users

QuickBooks Enterprise

This version of QuickBooks is designed for an organization that is large enough to have a small accounting department. It seeks to cater for slightly larger businesses than the other versions and provides the organization with a bigger data set. Here are some of its additional features:

- It has a 100,000 inventory limit

- It is able to support up to 30 users at once

- It enables management of employees and fixed assets

- It can be integrated into other business systems

The license fees are not beyond the reach of an average small business owner. It might cost anything from $5000 to $10,000 annually. If your company is still small, go for the Pro or Premier version, but as it grows larger, you should consider upgrading to the Enterprise accounting software.

Which QuickBooks Version Should You Buy?

The information provided above has given you the understanding of the different versions available, their features, pros, and cons. When it comes to narrowing down which one to choose for your business, you have to ask yourself a series of questions:

Does your business use Macs?

If your business relies on Mac software, then it is best to buy QuickBooks Mac or use QuickBooks Online. Alternatively, if you have a Mac computer but want to use QuickBooks Pro or Premier, you can still do so. The only issue is that you will have to use these versions within a Windows emulator, which will increase your support costs.

Does your business handle a lot of general accounting functions?

QuickBooks Pro is considered the workhorse accounting software of all the various versions available. It can handle a large volume of the daily bookkeeping tasks that any small business deals with. It is also very user-friendly.

Do you run your business on-the-go or remotely?

If you want to be able to access your files anywhere and at any time, choose QuickBooks Online. It is perfectly suited for a company that is fast-moving and can be run from any location. There is also the option of choosing QuickBooks Pro, which now comes with a mobile data and remote access. However, this option will incur your business an extra monthly charge on top of the license fee.

Do you need a version that is specific to your industry?

If you would prefer an option that makes it easier to maneuver according to the industry your business operates in, go for QuickBooks Premier. It will provide all the features tailored for your industry, for example, increased invent controls.

Does your business need to track inventory for both raw materials and finished products?

QuickBooks Pro would normally be a good fit for most businesses, but unfortunately, it does not provide adequate inventory tracking. For a business that handles a lot of inventory of raw material as well as finished products, QuickBooks Premier would be the way to go. It has all the features necessary for such an enterprise.

Chapter 4: Navigating Through QuickBooks

Navigating your way through QuickBooks shouldn't be a complicated process. There's a reason why QuickBooks is the most widely used accounting program in the market. Most small businesses that don't have a CPA or accounting team on staff have to do their own bookkeeping. QuickBooks is the obvious option because setting it up and navigating its many functions is quick and easy.

In this chapter, you will learn how to get started with QuickBooks, as well as how to customize and populate the myriad of lists and settings your company will need.

Getting Started With QuickBooks

If you are using QuickBooks for the first time, use this step-by-step guide to help you navigate through the setup:

Purchase and installation

It is assumed that you have already downloaded your QuickBooks desktop program from Intuit.com or bought an installation CD from some other third-party vendor. Follow the installation instructions on the screen and provide any information that the software will need to install on your computer.

QuickBooks registration

Once the installation is complete, QuickBooks asks you whether you want to register. Registering for QuickBooks packages can be done within a few minutes. You will need to provide some standard information to register your QuickBooks software, including your name, email, username, password, and how you plan on using the program.

If you are using QuickBooks Online, you will need to provide your credit card information. However, if you are using a free trial, you will not need a credit card. Whatever version or package you may want to use, there is always a free trial available. Free subscriptions can be used for 30 days, allowing you full unrestricted access for that period.

Customizing your account settings and business preferences

Once you have registered, you will need to set up your company preferences. On the menu bar at the top of the window, click on the **Company** menu and then choose **Preferences**. Edit the contact details for your company. You may want to change your account settings, for example, credit card payments, payroll and time tracking, or invoice automation. If you are using QuickBooks Online, you do not have to go through all this before using the program. You can choose to edit these settings later.

Importing your business data

You can import your business data from other QuickBooks programs. You can also import directly from bank account transactions, email apps, or Excel charts. On the top of the window, click on the **Company** menu, select **More**, and then from the drop-down menu, click on **Import Data**.

There's a lot of data that you can import into QuickBooks, such as:

- Excel chart of accounts

- Excel products and services

- QuickBooks desktop business data

- Vendor or client data from Gmail, Outlook, or Excel

- Bank transaction files

To import data, simply upload your XLS file, match every field with your QuickBooks fields, and then review the accuracy of the data. If you encounter any error messages, just make sure that your information is as specific as possible.

Importing contacts

Importing your business contacts into QuickBooks is easy. Click on the **Company** menu, choose **More**, and then click on **Import Data**. Click on **Vendors** or

Customers, depending on what kind of contact you want to import. Make sure that the customer or vendor data in your CSV or Excel files is split into vertical columns, i.e. name, address, and phone number in separate vertical columns. This will ensure that Quick Books sorts the information properly.

Once the file has been imported into QuickBooks, the software will fill the data into distinct fields. Review your data to weed out any inconsistencies, and then click **Continue**. Go through the information to see if all your contacts have been imported successfully.

Synchronizing your company bank accounts with QuickBooks

This process will enable you to automatically connect QuickBooks to your bank accounts. At the top of the QuickBooks window, you will see a **Banking** menu. Click on this menu and then choose **Download Transactions**.

A window will pop up and you will be required to fill in your bank account details, for example, the name of the bank and your account number. Of course, you will be required to have registered for online banking, as you will need to provide a login name and password. QuickBooks will then import your company bank account transactions.

The process takes a few minutes, but once it is complete, you should spend some time linking client or vendor names to every transaction. This will help you in the future when you need to associate a specific account with credit or debit information.

Synchronizing your credit cards

You need to make sure that the credit card accounts that your business holds are reflected in QuickBooks. The program is able to automatically record your information, keep track of it, and make sure it is up-to-date.

Go to the top of the window, click on **Banking** menu, and then choose **More**. From the drop down menu, select **Registers**. Fill in a new account name and then click **OK**. Once the pop-up window appears, choose **Credit Card** account option. QuickBooks will then launch a setup wizard to guide you through the steps of syncing your credit cards.

Customizing and branding your invoices

Every business owner needs to consider customizing his or her invoices with the company logo and brand. A QuickBooks invoice that looks attractive will impress your customers and give your business a professional look.

There are certain things that QuickBooks allows you to change on your invoice, including layout, style, font, color, and size. To customize your invoices, go to the top menu bar and click on the **Customers** menu. Choose **Create Invoices**, and from the drop-down menu, pick the template that you want for your business.

The templates look similar in layout but you can make changes to suit your preferences. Click on the **Formatting** menu and go to **Customize Data Layout**. When the pop-up window appears, you will be allowed to change any settings that you wish.

Adding your business logo to your invoices is simple. Just click on **Create Invoices** menu, select **Customize Design and Layout**, and then choose **Customize Data Layout**. An **Additional Customization** window will appear, and at the bottom of this window, click the **Basic Customization Button**. Find the **Use Logo** checkbox, and once the window pops up, choose the file to upload.

Edit your logo and crop it if you have to. Your logo has to fit into a square, so make sure that it is appropriate in size. You can preview the image by clicking on the **Open** button. Save the image by clicking **OK**.

Chapter 5: Using QuickBooks 2016 for Business Accounting

In this chapter, you will discover the many uses and functionalities that QuickBooks can offer your business. If you have set up your QuickBooks company data file with all the relevant information you will need, then you are ready to proceed.

The best thing about QuickBooks as an accounting software is that it provides you with multiple options when entering information into your account. As you read the steps describing how to use certain features, you will notice that there are many shortcuts leading to the same result. QuickBooks is designed to help you get to where you are going fast and easily.

Recording a Sales Receipt

Before you record a sales receipt in your QuickBooks accounting program, the customer must first have paid the entire amount for the goods or services provided. Recording of sales receipts for products sold is one of the most complex types of cash sales. It is a bit more involving than recording sales receipts for a service your business has offered. The steps described below will show you how to record a sales receipt for products.

How to record a sales receipt for products

1. Go to the **Customers** menu and click on **Enter Sales Receipts**. You can also go to your **Home** page and click on the icon called **Create Sales Receipts**. Another way to go is via the **Customer Center**, and then choosing the customer you want. Click on **New Transactions**, and then **Sales Receipts**. All three options lead you to the Enter Sales Receipts window.

2. On the right side of the **Customer: Job** box, click the down arrow and scroll down the list to find the name of the customer or job you want.

3. Move to the **Date** text field by pressing the Tab keyboard button or using your mouse. Fill in the right date in the format required.

4. You can enter a sales number for your sales receipt, though this is optional. Move over to the **Sale No**. text field and change the number that QuickBooks automatically provides.

5. QuickBooks normally uses the customer's billing address entered in the Customer list to automatically fill in the **Sold To** address box. If necessary, change the address.

6. Go to the **Check No**. text field and fill in your customer's check number. In case you are being paid in cash rather than check, don't fill in the box.

7. Indicate the method of payment by going to the **Payment Method** box and clicking the down

arrow. Choose the payment method from the list provided. If what you want to use is not on the list, click on **Add New**. A **New Payment Method** dialog box will appear. Describe the payment method you want and click OK.

8. On your screen, you will see a list box containing a row specifying ***Item/Description/Tax/Qty/Rate/Amount***. Move your cursor to the **Item** field and choose the item you want from the drop-down list that appears. QuickBooks will automatically enter the corresponding details into the **Description** and **Rate** fields. Specify the quantity of items you sold in the **Qty** field. If there are other items sold, follow the same process and fill in the rows beneath.

9. You may want to include special items on your sales receipt. However, you should note that QuickBooks identifies anything that you enter into your sales receipt as an item being sold. For example, if you place shipment charges in the receipt, QuickBooks will prompt you to enter it as an item in the list. Since shipping charges is a special item, place your cursor in an empty row of the **Item** box, click the drop-down arrow, and choose the special item. Once QuickBooks fills in the **Description** and **Rate** boxes, amend the information.

10. When you initially set up your QuickBooks program and created your company file, you specified your tax information. This is the default tax QuickBooks uses when filling in your sales tax in the receipt. If the sales tax specified is OK, move on. If it isn't,

click inside the ***Tax*** box and enter the appropriate tax.

11. Click on the ***Memo*** tab to write yourself a memo describing the cash sale. The memo is for your benefit, not the customer's, as it doesn't appear on the printed sales receipt.

12. Print the receipt by clicking the ***Print*** button.

13. Save your sales receipt by clicking on the ***Save & New*** or ***Save & Close*** buttons.

How to track what customers owe your business

There are a number of ways to do this, and we shall start with the simplest.

1. Click on the ***Customer*** menu, and then choose ***Customer Center***.

2. Pick out a customer from the ***Customer & Jobs*** column, which is displayed on your left. A page will be displayed showing all the transactions associated with that customer, including money owed.

Another way to determine how much a customer owes is to use accounts receivable reports.

1. Click on the **Reports** menu and select **Customers & Receivables**.

2. QuickBooks will show you several reports detailing customer information and how much each one owes your business.

You can decide to print a statement and send a friendly reminder to those customers with outstanding balances.

1. Click on the **Customers** menu and select **Create Statements**.

2. On the dialog box that appears, specify which customers you require statements for and the date ranges that will be displayed on the statement.

3. Click **Email** or **Print**.

Preparing Invoices and Credit Memos

Once you have learned and understood how to set up your QuickBooks program for your business, preparing templates like invoices and credit memos will not be difficult. Described below is a step by step process of creating these two documents.

How to prepare an invoice

1. Go to the **Customers** menu at the top of the window. Click on the **Create Invoices** tab. This will open up the Create Invoices window.

2. On the upper right-hand corner of the window, you will see a **Template** drop-down list. Choose the type of template you want to use for your invoice. The default template shown on your screen will be determined by the business information you gave QuickBooks when setting up the program. You are also allowed to create your own invoice template from scratch.

3. From the **Customer: Job** drop-down list, choose and click on your customer and the job.

4. Assign a date for your invoice by pressing the **Tab** button on your keyboard until the cursor reaches the **Date** text box. Fill in the right date manually, or simply use the calendar located on the right side of the text box.

5. If necessary, you can provide an invoice number using the **Invoice** #text box.

6. Assign the **Bill To** and **Ship To** address as you desire. QuickBooks assigns these addresses from your Customer list.

7. In case your customer gave you a purchase order, use the purchase order number in the **P.O. Number** text box.

8. Click on the **Terms** drop-down menu and specify whatever payment terms you had agreed on.

9. In case you choose to keep an eye on sales according to sales representatives, click on the **Rep** drop-down tab. Choose **Add New**. QuickBooks then provides dialog boxes to guide you. If you already have a sales rep list, click **Lists**, then **Customer and Vendor Profile Lists**. Finally, click **Sales Rep List**.

10. If your shipping date is different from the invoice date, specify it. Also, specify the mode of shipping.

11. Determine the Free-On-Board (FOB) point. Use the **FOB** text box to specify this information. The FOB point identifies when ownership of the goods occurs, which party pays the freight charges and bears the risk of damage. If FOB is at your company, ownership, freight charges and risk is transferred to the buyer the moment the goods leave your premises. If the FOB point is at the destination, transfer of ownership occurs at the receiver's premises, and the seller carries the charges and risk.

12. Enter the details of the items you are selling. You will see a row of text boxes indicating the type of information is required. Shift your cursor to the top row of the text boxes and QuickBooks will automatically activate a drop-down list for that particular text box. Choose the item you need from the list.

13. If there are any special items you want to include, go to the **Code** text box and click on the drop-down list. Pick the special item.

14. If you wish, you can add a message for your customer. Click on the drop-down list on the side of the **Customer Message** text box. You can use a template message or create your own special message. Click on the **Add New** button and follow the QuickBooks prompts.

15. Choose the right sales tax by clicking on the **Tax** box drop-down list.

16. Print the invoices individually or you can print them in batches. Batch invoicing is explained in the next chapter. If you want to delay the printing, click on the **Print Later** box located at the top part of the **Create Invoices** window.

17. Click on the **Save** button at the bottom of the window.

How to prepare a credit memo

A credit memo is issued whenever a customer is owed a refund, maybe for damaged goods or an overcharge of some sort. The process is similar to that of creating an invoice. The steps described are specifically for a product credit memo. For professional or service credit memos, you will be required to fill in fewer fields.

1. Click on **Customers** menu, and then **Create Credit Memos/Refunds**.

2. Choose the customer and the corresponding job from the list displayed.

3. Shift your cursor to the **Date** box and pick the correct date.

4. You have the option of entering a credit memo number. You can use the suggestion offered by QuickBooks or change it to whatever you want.

5. The **Customer Address** is automatically filled in. It should be the same as the one used in the original invoice.

6. In case your customer returned the products, make sure to describe every item. Go to the **Item/Description/Tax/Qty/Rate/Amount** text boxes. Place your cursor in a box, click the drop-down arrow, and choose the item returned. QuickBooks then fills in the Description and Rate. Fill in all the boxes accordingly, and move to the next rows if there are additional products returned. Do not forget to adjust your inventory list if products are returned.

7. Choose the sales tax.

8. If necessary, add a memo to explain why you are issuing a credit memo. This will print in the **Customer Statement**.

9. Print the credit memo or click on **Print Later**.

10. Save the credit memo by clicking on **Save & New** or **Save & Close**. You will be prompted to refund the money, retain the credit, or apply the credit to an invoice. Click on your preferred option.

Entering Credit Card Transactions

When you go to the **Banking** menu, click on **Register**, and choose a credit card account, the **Credit Card** register will be displayed. You then record charges by entering transactions within the blank rows. QuickBooks will then update your credit limit and credit card balance.

How to record a credit card charge

1. Click on the **Banking** menu and then choose **Enter Credit Card Charges**.

2. On the window displayed, go to the **Credit Card** field and click on the drop-down arrow in the box. Choose the credit card, which you used to pay for the expense.

3. Go to the **Purchased From** field and place your cursor in the box. Click on the drop-down arrow and select the name of the vendor you bought from. If you have never used the services of that vendor before, you will have to add it to the list. In the list displayed, click **Add New** and enter the name of the vendor.

4. Click on the **Purchase/Charge** button to record the purchase. In case you want to record money coming into your account due to a refund, click on the **Refund/Credit** button.

5. To enter the date when the charge was made, click in the **Date** field and type in the date. Always enter

the charge date and not the date when you recorded the charge. This will make your work easier when reconciling the credit card statement and your own records.

6. Place your cursor in the **Amount** field and fill in the total amount you were charged. Avoid typing a currency sign, but ensure that you place the period indicating where the decimal should be.

7. You can type a memo to describe the purpose of the item charged. Go to the **Memo** text field and enter the reason for the expense. For example, if you paid for dinner with the company credit card, type "*business meeting.*" This is important for tax purposes.

8. Go ahead and click on the **Expenses** tab. This is where you should always record your business expenses. In the Account column, click the drop-down arrow and pick an account from the list displayed. The list is populated with expense accounts that you created when you were setting up QuickBooks and syncing your credit cards (as described in the previous chapter). If you type in an account name that QuickBooks does not recognize, the program prompts you to create a new expense account.

9. At this point, you need to fill in the **Items** field. If the expense was a consumable product, for example, dinner at a restaurant, there is no need to itemize the charge. On the other hand, if you used the credit card to purchase supplies, timber, or other tangible things, you have to enter information

into the Items tab. In case there is a purchase order (PO) on record from the vendor whose name you entered in Step 3, the program will alert you. Click on the **Select Purchase Order** button to view a list of outstanding POs from that particular vendor.

10. To record the charge in the Credit Card register, click on **Save & New** or **Save & Close**.

How to correct a mistake in your credit card charge

If you discover that you made an error when entering a credit card charge, or need to delete it altogether, follow the steps below:

1. Click on the **Lists** tab and select **Chart of Accounts**. A window will open up.

2. Identify the credit card account that contains the wrong charge. Double-click on it. This will open the **Credit Card** register window.

3. Choose which transaction to alter or delete by moving the cursor to it.

4. You have three options here: void, delete, or edit. If you want to void the transaction, click **Edit**, then **Void Credit Card Charge,** then **OK**. To delete, click **Edit**, then **Delete Credit Card Charge**, and then **OK**. To edit, click **Edit Transaction**, which is in the top part of the window. This will open the window **Enter Credit Card Charges.** Edit

whatever needs changing and then save your changes by clicking the appropriate **Save** button.

Filling Out Purchase Orders

Whenever your business runs out of an item, it's time to order some more. This means you have to write a purchase order. QuickBooks enables you to do this using the following easy steps:

1. There are three different routes to creating a purchase order. You can click on the **Vendors** tab and select **Create Purchase Orders**. You could also go to your **Home** page and click on the **Purchase Orders** icon. Alternatively, you can go to the **Vendor Center**, click on **New Transactions**, and then choose **Purchase Orders**.

2. On the **Vendor** field, click the drop-down arrow on the right to display a list of vendors. Click on the vendor you want to display the name and address. If the vendor is not on the list, you can add them by clicking on the **Add New** option, which is on the list. When the New Vendor dialog box opens, enter the relevant information and then click **OK**.

3. If you had designed your purchase order to include additional fields like **Expected Date**, **Rep**, or **FOB**, fill them in with relevant information.

4. In the **Item** column, fill in the items that you want to order. Click the drop-down arrow to display a list

of items, and scroll through to pick items. You can choose as many items as you need. In case the item is not in the list, QuickBooks will prompt you to set it up. Click on **Set Up** and enter the required details in the **New Item** window. When you enter an item, the Description column is automatically filled, but you can edit this information. If you adjust the cost of an item, the program will ask you whether the new cost should be updated to be the standard cost for that particular item. Click on either **Yes** or **No**, and then click **OK**.

5. You can decide to include a message to the vendor by entering your message in the **Vendor Message** field. The vendor message could be a note declaring the urgency for delivery of your order. You should also write a message for yourself in the **Memo** field. This will help you recall what the purchase order was for when paying for items received later on.

6. The **Create Purchase Orders** screen contains a check box titled **Print Later**. Clicking this box activates the check mark and prints your purchase order. Once the purchase order has been printed, the check mark vanishes.

7. Click the **Print** button to print the purchase order. In case you have several purchase orders that you need to print together, click the drop-down arrow under the **Print** tab and choose **Preview**. Once you are satisfied with the look of the purchase order, click the arrow again and select **Batch**.

8. To record your purchase order, click on the **Save** button – **Save & New** or **Save & Close**.

Payroll Management

This section covers how to create a payroll item, which is essentially anything that alters how much someone is paid. You have the option of setting up payroll manually or outsourcing this function to a QuickBooks payroll service. You will learn how to do both. It is recommended that you do not set up payroll manually if you are currently subscribed to a payroll service.

Setting up manual payroll

1. In the QuickBooks homepage, click on **Help** menu, and then **QuickBooks Help**.

2. Click on the **Search** tab and write "manual payroll" in the text box. Press **Enter**.

3. Click on the topic titled **Calculate payroll taxes manually (without a subscription to QuickBooks Payroll)**.

4. Click on **Manual Payroll Calculations**, which appears under **Set your company file to use the manual payroll calculations** setting.

5. Go to the link **Set my company file to use manual calculations**.

6. Now close and reopen your QuickBooks program.

7. In case you discover that your payroll features are not showing when you click on the **Employees** menu, you need to check your preferences.

8. Go to the top of the window and click on the **Edit** menu.

9. Choose **Preferences**.

10. Click on **Payroll & Employees**.

11. Select the **Company Preferences** option.

12. Click on **Full Payroll** and then **OK**.

Subscribing to a QuickBooks payroll service

The cost of subscribing to Intuit QuickBooks Payroll service will depend on how many employees work in your company, as well as how many functions you choose to outsource to Intuit. If you want to use the most basic package, you could spend at least $200 every year. The full service usually costs a minimum of $1000 every year. To subscribe to a payroll service, connect to the Internet and follow these steps:

1. Click on the **Employees** menu, go to **Payroll**, and then choose **Order Payroll Service**. You will be directed to a web form where you will be asked to sign up and select the type of **QuickBooks Payroll Service** you need. You can choose the Basic Payroll service or the Enhanced Payroll service. In Basic Payroll, QuickBooks will work on your checks but your bookkeeper will have to do the filing of the tax returns. In Enhanced Payroll, QuickBooks does all the work for you, checks as well as payroll tax forms.

2. Follow the instructions and prompts carefully. The process is quick and easy if you have all the necessary information from the start – around 30 minutes. You need to have precise year-to-date payroll information of all employees. You also need information about your state's withholding rate.

3. Once you have set up your QuickBooks Payroll service, it is time to schedule any upcoming payroll activities. Click on the **Employees** menu, and then choose **Add or Edit Payroll Schedules**. A window called **Payroll Schedule List** will pop up. Click on **Payroll Schedule** button and then select **New**. QuickBooks will prompt you to give further details about your scheduled payroll. If it's a weekly payroll, you may describe the payroll as "Friday payroll."

4. Finally, you need to describe your company's employees according to the payroll schedule assigned to them. Click on the **Employees** menu, and then select **Employee Centre**. Click on **New Employee** and fill in your employee's details in the tabs of the pop-up window displayed. Please use the **Payroll and Compensation** menu to spell out wages for every employee and assign everyone to a payroll schedule.

Recording Bills and Writing Checks

Whenever a bill is received from a vendor, it must first be recorded in your QuickBooks accounting program. This can be done either via the **Accounts Payable** register or the **Enter Bills** window. The Enter Bills option allows you to track your incoming bills according to item and expense, and this is the option that is described below.

How to record your bills

1. On your Home Page, go to the **Vendors** area and click on **Enter Bills**. The window that is displayed resembles a check because most of the details you fill in here will be used on the check that you will issue for paying your bill.

2. Click on the drop-down arrow at the **Vendor** line to display your list of vendors. Select the vendor whom you are paying from the list of existing vendors. If they are a new vendor, you will have to click on **Quick Add** and fill in the vendor information such as name, address, payment terms, credit limit, et cetera.

3. Go to the **Terms** menu and click on the drop-down arrow. Select payment terms, for example, when the bill is due.

4. Type in the vendor's reference number. This could be the invoice number and will be printed on the check.

5. You can also enter a memo in the **Memo** text box, though this is not necessary.

6. Click on the **Expenses** tab and go to the **Account** column. If the name of the expense account that the bill represents already exists in your chart of

accounts, click the drop-down arrow and choose the account. If it is a new expense account, go to the top of the list and click on **Add New**. A **New Account** dialog box will open. Fill in the details. If you have multiple expense accounts and want to split the bill among them, just click the new account you've created. When a drop-down arrow appears, click it and enter the next expense account.

7. If you have split the bill, ensure that the individual amounts add up to the bill total. Check the **Amount** column.

8. You can write a message in the **Memo** column. (Optional)

9. Click on the **Items** menu and fill in the information about the items purchased and their rates. Use the drop-down arrow in the **Vendor** tab to choose the vendor who billed you.

10. Find the drop-down arrow next to the Items tab. Click the arrow and see if the item is on the list. If it is, select that item. If it isn't, scroll upwards on the list and click **Add New,** and then enter details into the **New Item** window.

11. Use the **Items** tab to enter every item you are buying, their cost, and quantities. Use the **Recalculate** button to add up the costs.

12. Click on **Save and New** to record another bill or **Save and Close** to exit.

How to pay your bills

1. Click on the **Vendors** menu and then select **Pay Bills**. Another way is to click on the Pay Bills tab on your home page.

2. At the bottom of the window, you will notice the date indicated as today's date. Change the **Payment Date** as you want it to be displayed on the check.

3. Go to the **Show Bills Due On or Before** date field and specify the date. Select **Show All Bills** if you want all bills to be displayed.

4. Click on the **Sort By** drop-down arrow to enable QuickBooks to arrange the bills according to whatever specifications you want.

5. Pick the bills you want to pay by clicking on the left side of the bill's due date. You can also click the **Select All Bills** button to pay all the bills.

6. If you want to pay only part of a bill, change the figure in the **Amount to Pay** column.

7. You may choose to use your credit memos to pay off some of the bills. Click the Set Credits tab. Look at the list of credits in the **Discount and Credits** dialog box. Click on the credit memo you want to use and then click **Done**.

8. On the **Payments** menu, go to the **Date** field and specify the payment date. Click on the drop-down list beside the **Method** tab to choose the payment method. Click on the drop-down arrow next to **Accounts** tab to pick the bank account to be used

to release the funds. In case you have subscribed to QuickBooks online payment, you can pay via the Internet.

9. You can print the check by clicking the **To Be Printed** button. Alternatively, if the checks will be written by hand later, click the **Assign Check Number** button. Type the number or let QuickBooks assign its own number.

10. To pay your bills, click the **Pay Selected Bills** button. A Payment summary dialog box opens where you can review a list of all the bills paid. Click on the **Pay More Bills** tab to select more bills for payment. You can also move forward and print checks by clicking the **Print Checks** button. One thing to note is that after you have paid a bill, QuickBooks records this transaction in the Accounts Payable register. The program then writes the check, ready for delivery to the payee.

Creating Reports in QuickBooks

One of the many benefits of using QuickBooks is that it allows you to generate a number of different reports that you can use to view the status of your company. This information is presented in a format that any business owner can read easily and understand. QuickBooks also comes with inbuilt reports, though you can create your own to suit your specific needs.

How to create a report

1. Go to the **Reports** menu on your Home page.

2. Click on the type of report to be created. There are different categories of reports provided, such as **Inventory**, **Customers**, and **Sales**. Choose your report according to the kind of information you need to view.

3. Under the given categories, there are also sub-categories that are more explicit, for example, Balance Sheet.

4. Once you have selected the specific type of report you want, click on **Modify Report**, which is located at the top section of the window. Go ahead and choose **Display**.

5. In the bottom part of the window, go to **Columns** area and choose which columns to add or delete from your report.

6. Go to the **Report Date Range** area and choose the date range.

7. QuickBooks allows you to choose the filters to apply in your report. At the top of your window, find the **Filters** tab and click on it. Select your filters, for example, the types of accounts you want to include in the report.

8. Click on the **OK** button.

How to modify reports

The Report window that QuickBooks displays has a toolbar containing a number of buttons. One of these is the **Customize Report** button, which helps you modify your reports as needed.

1. Click on the **Customize Report** tab. QuickBooks will open a **Modify Report** window.

2. Use the open window to edit or modify whatever information that is to be shown in your report. Click on the **Display** tab to modify how information will be arranged.

3. Click on the **Filters** tab to change the data that will be used to generate your report.

4. Click on the **Header/Footer** tab to change the header and footer details.

5. Click on the **Fonts & Numbers** tab to set the size of print to be used as well as the typeface for the report.

6. When you are done, click the **OK** button at the bottom.

Balancing Your Bank Account

QuickBooks makes the process of balancing your bank account very simple. This process involves comparing transactions recorded in the end-month bank statements with those listed in your business accounting records. This is also known as reconciliation. Reconciliation should take place at least once every month. Any discrepancies between the two accounts should be cause for concern.

Here are the steps for balancing your bank account:

1. You need to provide QuickBooks with the necessary information regarding your bank account information. Click on the **Banking** menu and select **Reconcile**. Alternatively, go to your home page and click on the Reconcile tab. The **Begin Reconcile** dialog box will open up. In case your business has more than one bank account, click the **Account** tab and choose the account you need to reconcile.

2. Pick the date of the bank statement by filling in the **Statement Date** text field. Alternatively, use the Calendar button on the side of the text box.

3. Confirm that the opening balance written in your bank statement is correct by comparing it to that in the **Beginning Balance** text box.

4. Take your ending balance from your bank statement and type it into the **Ending Balance** text box in QuickBooks.

5. Look for the bank service charge in your statement. Go to the **Service Charge** text box and enter this service charge.

6. Provide the correct transaction date for the above service charge.

7. On the side of the **Date** text field, you will see an **Account** text box. Click on the drop-down arrow to assign the service charge to a specific account.

8. Go to the **Interest Earned** text field and enter the interest earned by the account over the last month. Provide a transaction date for the interest earned.

9. Go to the second **Account** text field and provide the account, which you will assign the interest earned.

10. Click on the **Continue** tab. QuickBooks will bring up the Reconcile window showing a split-screen of transactions – **Checks and Payments** window on the left and **Deposits and Other Credits** on the right.

How to mark cleared checks and deposits

In this process, you use the Reconcile window in QuickBooks to verify the amounts against your bank statements. Take the following steps to inform QuickBooks which checks and deposits tally with the bank statement:

1. Find the first deposit, which has cleared. Go through the list of transactions in the **Deposits and Other Credits** window and click on the corresponding deposit. A check mark is placed on the left side of the deposit transaction to indicate that it is cleared. The balance statement is also cleared.

2. In case there is a deposit missing in the Reconcile window, it means that you did not enter it into the

register. Click the **Leave** button to close the Reconcile window. Go to the register and feed in the required information as normal. Alternatively, go to the **Banking** menu, click on **Make Deposits**, and record the deposit. **Save and Close**. When you reopen the Reconcile window, you should see the new deposit displayed in the **Deposits and Other Credits** window.

3. Repeat the above steps for every deposit that appears on your bank statement. Ensure that the dates and amounts tally. If there is an error, correct it. Click on the **Save and Close** button.

4. On your bank statement, look for the first check that is listed.

5. In the Reconcile window, click on the column headings to sort through the transactions. Scroll through the Checks and Payments list to identify the first check, which was cleared. Mark the check by clicking on it. The transaction is then cleared and the statement balance updated.

6. Use steps 4 and 5 to reconcile the withdrawals in the bank statement.

Reasons for mismatch between your QuickBooks records and bank statement

There are times when your accounting records will fail to reconcile with your bank statements, even though no mistakes have been made. Here are a few reasons why:

1. Outstanding checks

It may be possible that checks you have issued to creditors have not been cashed yet. Your internal records will reflect the money as paid but it may still be sitting in your bank account. It may also be possible that you have received payment from a customer yet the amount hasn't been cleared by your bank, thus reflecting in your QuickBooks records but not on your bank balance sheet.

2. Bank fees

When the bank debits your account as bank fees, this transaction is not recorded in your internal bookkeeping records. This is also true for interest that your deposit earns.

What to do when your accounts fail to balance

1. Check whether any mistakes were made in recording interest on loan repayments, interest earned on deposits or bank fees.

2. Check our bank statement to confirm whether every transaction listed has been cleared in your QuickBooks account. A transaction that was reconciled could have been inadvertently deleted or unchecked.

3. Cross-check your bank statement and your QuickBooks records to make sure that there are no missing checks or deposits transactions.

Job Costing/Estimates

The first step of job costing in QuickBooks is coming up with an estimate. An estimate refers to a list of the potential costs that your business will incur when undertaking a job for a client. If you have created a job in QuickBooks and set up the program to use estimates, follow these steps to create a job estimate.

How to create a job estimate

1. Click on the **Customers** menu, and then select **Estimates**. QuickBooks will open a form that looks like the one used when making an invoice.

2. On the top part of the form, click on the drop-down arrow and pick the right **Customer: Job**. QuickBooks will automatically add in the rest of the details into the form, for example, the name and address. You are allowed to change the default settings for the date and estimate number.

3. Fill in the details in the **Create Estimates** window. This information is similar to what goes into an invoice.

4. Every line item within a job estimate has to be fully described in the **Items** list. This is for the benefit of the customer you are trying to sell to. The clearer your job estimate is, the better, as it helps them understand exactly what they are paying for.

5. QuickBooks allows you to add a message or memo in your estimate. Click on the drop-down list in the **Customer Message** field to use one of the pre-programmed messages. Alternatively, you can create your own customized message. You may also write a memo to yourself by using the **Memo** tab.

6. If you need to customize your estimate further, you should click on the **Formatting** menu to display the formatting ribbon. Click the **Customize Data Layout** tab and QuickBooks will show a dialog box for tweaking the details that are displayed in your estimate.

7. Please note that the information you have entered on your **Create Estimates** window is not what will be printed out in your estimate. The printed version can be viewed by going to the bottom of the **Print** button and clicking the drop-down arrow. Select **Preview**.

8. If you want to print the estimate, click on the Print button. A dialog box will appear requesting to **Print One Estimate**. Click **Print**.

9. Click on either **Save & New** or **Save & Close**.

Charging Customers for Time and Costs

Before you invoice a customer for a job you have performed, you first have to track the time spent on the job and the costs incurred.

How to track time

The time spent working on a customer's job can be tracked as follows:

1. Click on the **Edit** menu, and then select **Preferences**.

2. Scroll downwards and click on the **Time and Expenses** menu. Under company preferences, select **Do You Track Time** option.

3. Track and record a customer's time by clicking on the **Customers** tab, then **Enter Time**, followed by **Use Weekly Timesheet**. This will allow you to record how much time you spend working for a specific client. NB: The clock used to track time keeps running only when the QuickBooks software is being used. With the newer versions of QuickBooks, the timer does not stop even if you minimize the window and start working on another program, such as Excel or Outlook.

How to charge a customer for costs and time

1. Click the **Customers** menu and select **Create Invoices**.

2. In the Create Invoices window, click on the drop-down arrow in the **Customer: Job** tab. From the list displayed, pick the proper customer name and job.

3. In the event you had allocated costs or time to the selected customer, a pop-up window will appear, requesting you to click on the **Costs/Time** button. Doing so will input the charges into your invoice.

4. Click the Add Time/Costs tab. A dialog box will pop up. Click on the **Billable Time and Costs** option.

5. Choose the billable costs and times that you want to appear on your invoice. Make sure that the information that you add to the invoice is accurate. The dialog box that opened contains multiple tabs – for Items, Mileage, and Expenses.

6. If you want to add expenses into the invoice, you will have to indicate your markup. Enter the required information into the **Markup %** and **Markup Account** fields.

7. Click the **OK** button.

8. If you want to see which job costs appear in the invoice, go to the **Print** button and click on the drop-down arrow. Select **Preview**.

9. Record the invoice by clicking on the **Save & Close** button.

10. Once an invoice is recorded, the job costs that were previously billed are instantly removed from the Choose Billable Time and Costs window.

Managing Your Company Data Files

It is critical for your business for you to regularly back up data files. You should never go for more than a day without backing up your company accounting files because data loss can be a real nightmare for your business. Fortunately, QuickBooks makes data backup very easy. It enables you to set reminders, verifies the integrity of your data, and allows regularly scheduled backups.

There are two methods of data backup in QuickBooks: manual and automatic.

How to back up files manually

1. Click on the *File* menu and then select *Back Up*.

2. Go to the *Back Up Company File* menu and click on it.

3. Click on the *Browse* button to enter an appropriate name for the file and also to specify the backup location.

4. Click on the *Save* button.

5. If there are other files to be backed up, use the *Back Up Options* menu.

6. Click on *OK*.

How to back up files automatically

QuickBooks normally backs up your data every time you close the file. The program allows you to determine how frequently this backup is created. The backup file is stored on the computer's hard drive, in a QuickBooks directory folder called "Auto Backup."

1. Go to the **File** menu and click on the **Backup** tab.

2. Select the **Schedule a Backup** button.

3. Click on the box named **Automatically back up when closing data file every**. You will then have to choose the frequency of your backups.

4. On the **QuickBooks Backup** screen, choose your preferred selections.

5. Click on the **OK** button.

Another method by which QuickBooks allows you to back up automatically is through Scheduled Unattended Backup. Unlike the backup described above, you don't even need to be at your computer for the backup to occur. However, the data file has to be closed when the backup is going on.

1. Go to the **File** menu and click on the **Back Up** button.

2. Choose the **Schedule Backup** button.

3. Click on the **New** button.

4. Use the **Schedule Backup** screen to choose your preferred backup options.

5. To save the backup schedule, click on the **OK** button.

How to use audit trails

If you have a number of employees within your company who have access to the QuickBooks data file, you must learn how to use audit trails. QuickBooks contains an audit trail feature that helps you to track every employee who alters data in the data file. Every specific change that is made is also recorded. The transactions recorded on the Audit Trail report cannot be removed easily unless you archive and condense the data.

The Audit Trail Tracking feature is always turned on. QuickBooks ensures that your data files are always under scrutiny so that you can quickly identify who altered some information and when this was done.

QuickBooks also allows you view a comprehensive Audit Trail report. To generate this report, follow these easy steps:

1. Click on the **Reports** menu.

2. Click on the **Accountant and Taxes** button.

3. From the submenu provided, choose **Audit Trail**. The report will appear on your screen.

Chapter 6: QuickBooks Tips and Tricks

QuickBooks is very popular and widely used by most small businesses. However, there are some features of this accounting program that are not being fully or efficiently utilized. Even your average CPA may not be aware of some of the strongest features that QuickBooks offers. If you want your business to make the most out of QuickBooks rather than simply relying on the basic features everybody knows about, you have to understand the shortcuts, tips, and tricks that you can use.

Here are some intermediate and advanced QuickBooks features that you should definitely learn how to use.

Memorizing Transactions

Every business has a significant number of transactions that are constantly recurring. Rather than trying to remember these transactions, use QuickBooks to automatically memorize these regular transactions. For example, if your business pays rent on a specific date every month, or you bill a customer for a monthly service, QuickBooks automatically memorizes them and helps you fill in the related information at programmed intervals. This feature enables you to save time, minimize errors, and improve accuracy. If you have complicated journal entries and templates that you have to remember, use this feature to make life easier.

To make use of this memorizing transaction tool, use the keyboard shortcut ***Ctrl + M***. Though the memorize transaction tool creates electronic payments, it does not send them automatically. You can send documents by going to ***File*** menu and clicking on ***Send Documents***.

QuickBooks Loan Manager

When it comes to recording loan repayment transactions, the majority of small business owners do not follow the correct process. Businesses fail to follow the loan repayment schedule by forgetting to separate the principal amounts and the loan interest accrued. QuickBooks makes loan repayment management easier by helping you set up every individual loan according to its related parameters. The QuickBooks Loan Manager tool makes sure the loan rate, term, balloon payments, compounding, and fees are filled in correctly every time. It then generates an accurate payment check every time a loan repayment is due. This not only reduces errors but also saves time.

To make use of this tool, click on ***Banking***, and then ***Loan Manager***.

Processing Multiple Reports

For a business to be managed effectively, it is important for the company personnel to have in their possession the relevant financial reports. In most cases, bookkeepers maintain the records well but then fail to generate and distribute these reports on a consistent basis. This is usually because preparing and printing all these reports takes too much time. To make this process easier, QuickBooks contains a tool known as *Process Multiple Reports*. This tool works together with the *Memorize* function and helps you create and print a batch of multiple reports at the click of a button.

To make use of this tool, click on the **Reports** tab, then go to **Process Multiple Reports**. One trick you can use is to add the name of the recipient in the title of the report when memorizing every report. This will make the report distribution process much easier.

Avoiding Prior-Period Changes

QuickBooks make it very easy for users to enter and edit transactions. Unfortunately, sometimes a user can unintentionally make a change in a prior period. To prevent such errors from occurring, you need to set up a special username and password for every person who uses the system, as well as set preferences for each user to stop them bypassing the closing date.

Once you have set up a closing date that is password protected, all you have to do is move the closing date forward each month as adjustments are made. To make use of this tip, click on the **Company** menu, and then **Set Closing Date**.

Custom Data Fields

This feature can be considered as one of accounting software's most powerful features. Depending on the version of QuickBooks you are using, you have the option of between 20 to 50 generic custom data fields, each field being content-specific. Data fields are very handy when it comes to overcoming the many shortcomings that an accounting system has. If for instance, you are running a boat rental service in a marina, you can use custom data fields to keep track of a client, the details of the boat they rented, the slip number where they have parked, and whether they subscribe to your monthly cranking service.

More than that, QuickBooks provides you with the option of filtering reports using your custom data fields. For instance, your boat rental service could easily determine how many boats need cranking every month. This can be done by filtering the customer records to show only those who have a subscription for the cranking service.

To make use of this tool, click on the **Customer Center** tab, choose a specific **Customer**, and go to **Edit**

Customer. Click on the ***Additional Information*** tab and select ***Define Fields***. Another tip about this QuickBooks feature is that you can include the information generated by Custom Data within an invoice, financial report, or any QuickBooks document.

Batch Invoicing

QuickBooks allows you to generate multiple invoices at a go. For instance, if you want to send invoices to your 1000 clients every month, you can easily create 1000 invoices in one process. QuickBooks' batch invoicing feature also enables you to find specific customers according to custom data fields, and then invoice that select group.

Using the example of the boat rental service, the accountant would be able to send invoices to all the customers who have signed up for the monthly cranking service –all in one step. To make use of this tool, go to ***Customers*** menu, and click on the ***Create Batch Invoices*** tab at the bottom of the screen.

Editing Templates

 In QuickBooks, all types of documents are referred to as templates, whether it is an invoice, statement, purchase order, or sales order. QuickBooks makes it possible for you to change these templates by rearranging the structure of a document. If you need to include some extra information such as additional columns, images, data fields, or text, you can do so easily.

For instance, you may decide to include your sales agent's name and telephone number in a company invoice. You may also decide to add extra columns to show information like rates and quantities. All this is possible by using the Editing Templates functionality. Any smart business owner will see the need to tweak their templates to effectively meet their business goals.

To make use of this tool, click on the **Lists** menu and go to **Templates**. You will see several template options. Right-click on a template, select **Edit Template,** and then click on the **Layout Designer** tab. You can also choose to download extra templates and colorful themes from the Internet if you wish.

Chapter 7: The Common QuickBooks Errors To Avoid

There is no accounting software that has gained as much popularity since its inception as QuickBooks. This software solution is perfectly designed for small businesses to handle all their accounting requirements in one place.

QuickBooks has proven itself extremely useful for small businesses especially when it comes to maintaining financial records. It provides businesses with the ability to manage inventory, payroll, and sales, as well as several other critical financial items.

In this chapter, you will learn about the most common mistakes that a QuickBooks user can commit. In most cases, business owners don't really set up QuickBooks correctly to suit their company's needs. Some businesses even end up using a QuickBooks version that is completely wrong for their type of business. When this happens, a business owner then spends a lot of time and money trying to find someone to help them fix their QuickBooks file.

As explained earlier, there are different versions of QuickBooks that you can use, and it is crucial that you understand how each one accumulated data. This will help you avoid mistakes. These mistakes can range from setup errors, procedural errors, and many other general errors that any small business may commit.

Listed below are the 15 most common mistakes made when using QuickBooks and how to avoid them:

Mistake #1: Constraining QuickBooks to a Bookkeeping Tool Instead of a Financial Driver

There are so many financial functions of QuickBooks yet most business owners just want to use the software for basic bookkeeping. QuickBooks allows you to create a budget and even track how you spend money in relation to that budget. You also have the option of reviewing your business' financial reports, for example, balance sheet and profit and loss account. You can also customize your own reports to reflect what you want to keep track of, for example, profitability, accounts payable, and receivables aging.

Mistake #2: Forgetting To Set Sales Tax Preferences

Your business may be selling items that attract a sales tax, and this means that you have to set up the sales tax preferences in QuickBooks. If you omit this process, your records will not be accurate. In order to set up your sales tax preferences, follow this procedure: Click on **Edit**, then **Preferences**. Click the **Sales Tax** icon, and go to

Company Preferences. Click on **Owe Sales Tax** and then choose one of the two options available – either Upon Receipt of Payment or As of Invoice Date.

Mistake #3: Creating Too Many Accounts and Sub-Accounts

This is one error that is very tempting to make. You may think that creating multiple accounts and sub-accounts will make maintaining financial records easier, but it will not. What results is actually an overly complicated system that will be prone to mistakes. One of the greatest advantages that QuickBooks provides is offering a business the option of creating accounts and sub-accounts. However, this does not mean you have to do so in a haphazard manner. Create an accounts information system that is logical and follows a coherent procedure. If need be, keep the accounts categories to a minimum.

Mistake #4: Not Reconciling Your Accounts

Your business accounts must always be reconciled in order to ensure that your account register is in proper order. Failure to reconcile QuickBooks accounts leads to messy balance sheets. Reconciling involves all the different accounts that your business operates, for example, loans, credit card, taxes, savings, and checking accounts. Reconciling your business accounts is what alerts you to any inconsistencies in any of your accounting records. To do this, go to the **Banking** section, click on the **Reconcile** tab, and fill in the statement dates as well as end balances. Once every item under the Checks and Payments section has been ticked off, you should see a zero reading on the bottom right-hand corner. This is something that you should be doing at least on a monthly basis.

Mistake #5: Making Loan Payments by Writing a Check or Entering a Bill

The majority of small businesses tend to make their monthly loan payments by using the Write a Check or Enter a Bill window. This is an exhausting way of paying back loans because it is cumbersome, manual, and open to mistakes. If you want to make loan payments for your business, it is recommended that you click on Banking, go to Loan Manager, and then choose Set Up Payment. This procedure will enable QuickBooks to automatically calculate every monthly loan payment your business owes while also keeping track of the interest accrued.

Mistake #6: Writing Checks Without Entering Bills

For most small businesses, any bill that arrives is handled by simply utilizing the **Write Check** feature. The business owner rushes to pay the bill but forgets to create an

Accounts Payable. The first thing that every business owner needs to do with every bill received is to enter it in the **Enter Bills** window. This step ensures that an Accounts Payable is created. You then click on **Pay Bills** and choose the bill that you want to pay. When you do this, the accounts payable associated with that particular vendor is taken care of. This gives you the freedom to use QuickBooks to adequately deal with the cash flow of your business while planning for any expenses that may occur in the future.

Mistake #7: Paying Payroll Taxes Through the Write Checks Window

One of the critical functions of QuickBooks when it comes to payroll processing is tracking how much money the business owes in payroll taxes. QuickBooks allows you to record your payroll tax in the Payment Liabilities window, but if you pay these taxes through the Write Checks window, the deduction will not be properly recorded in the Payment Liabilities window. You need to ensure that your business maintains straight financial books, so make sure that all your payroll taxes are paid directly via the Payroll Liability window.

Mistake #8: Incorrect Receipt of Payments

The majority of business owners tend to record any money received in the Make Deposits window. What you need to do, however, is record such payments in the Receive Payments screen. This way, QuickBooks will ensure that the invoice is shown as having been paid.

Mistake #9: Irregular Review of Balance Sheet and Profit & Loss Statements

Any business that does not regularly review its profit and loss accounts, as well as its balance sheet statement, is asking for trouble. Keeping your files updated may be a pain, but there is no escaping this crucial part of running a functional business. The balance sheet and profit and loss are the two statements that indicate the financial health of your business. They also help you detect any financial errors that may end up costing you a lot of money. It is extremely critical that these two statements be reviewed and updated on a regular basis. If you cannot do this by yourself, it would be wise to outsource this work. It is recommended that you update your QuickBooks files weekly, and you can make this easier by scheduling this activity just as you would any other appointment.

Mistake #10: Failing To Back Up Data

In life, you have to be aware that anything can happen at any time. Computers can crash suddenly, inadvertently wiping out your records and files. As a business owner, make sure that all your QuickBooks records and files are backed up every day. When the business day ends, ensure that you do not fail to save copies in an offline device, for example, flash drives.

Mistake #11: Using Obsolete Versions of QuickBooks

If you are using a desktop version of QuickBooks rather than the online one, you need to make sure that it is updated. QuickBooks no longer supports versions that are more than three years old. The updated versions provide your business with automatic downloads of bank and credit card transactions straight from the relevant institutions. The newer versions also enable you to bill several clients for recurring monthly fees.

Mistake #12: Failing To Expand the Capabilities of QuickBooks

Depending on the nature, size, and complexity of your business, there are times when you might need to expand the capabilities of your QuickBooks reporting files. Unfortunately, most small businesses tend to forget that there are apps, consolidation software, and add-ons that can make their lives easier. By expanding your QuickBooks capabilities, you will be able to handle the complicated aspects of your business financial records, especially if your business is growing. If your business has developed extra needs, it would be smart for you as a business owner to search for available software that will enable you to maximize your use of QuickBooks.

Mistake #13: Hiring an Incompetent Person

This is one mistake that is very common with small businesses, yet it has the ability to seriously affect the success of your business. When hiring a QuickBooks expert or consultant, make sure that you know the level of accounting and bookkeeping experience they have. Ask them detailed questions on how they would resolve specific accounting issues and challenges. There are a lot of outsourcing companies out there that can provide you with a competent QuickBooks expert, so there's no reason to make a mistake as this.

Mistake #14: Ignoring Shortcut Options

As a business owner, it is usually a struggle to find enough time to sit down and perform your bookkeeping and accounting roles. If manually typing and clicking your way through every transaction in the QuickBooks interface is your thing, that's OK. However, there are many shortcuts that you can use in QuickBooks to save you time and energy. Go to the QuickBooks help menu to find all the information you need on how to use the various shortcut keys.

Mistake#15: Over-Relying On Technology

It is one thing to invest heavily in accounting and bookkeeping technology, but something totally different to make that technology work properly. You also need to realize that not all technology is relevant for your business. As a small business owner, you do not have to put a lot of money into expensive and complex business accounting systems. You are better off using a QuickBooks version that will help you maintain financial statements and consider upgrading as your business grows. You have to be strategic and do research to find what works for you so that you don't end up with technology that simply exacerbates your accounting errors.

Conclusion

As a small business owner, you want to make sure that your company accounts are always in order, yet doing so may be costly and time-consuming. That's why you need QuickBooks accounting software. This book has provided you with a comprehensive overview of everything you need to understand how QuickBooks works, how to get started, and how to use the many great features QuickBooks offers.

If you feel that there is something you haven't understood, go back and read it again. It would be most beneficial if you have this book with you as you practice navigating through the program.

It is recommended that you first figure out which version of QuickBooks would serve your company the best. Use the criteria described here if you want to make the right choice and maximize your investment in QuickBooks.

Use the tips, tricks, and shortcuts explained in the book. They will save you a lot of time and energy. Finally, keep in mind that there are many potential mistakes that can be made. Always double check your work and read the book again to make sure you've done things the right way.

We hope that you will use all the information presented in this book to your advantage, and take your business to the next level!

QuickBooks
Resources

www.learnthat.com

www.journalofaccountancy.com

www.bebusinessed.com

www.dummies.com

www.agsci.psu.edu

Made in the USA
Lexington, KY
28 July 2017